WITHDRAWN

The Mystery of FORTUNE-TELLING

Carl R. Green and William R. Sanford

Enslow Publishers, Inc.
40 Industrial Road
Box 398
Berkeley Heights, NJ 07922
USA
http://www.enslow.com

MIDDLEBROOK MEDIA CENTER
WILTON, CT

Copyright © 2012 by Carl R. Green and William R. Sanford

All rights reserved.

No part of this book may be reproduced by any means
without the written permission of the publisher.

Original edition published as *Fortune Telling* in 1993.

Library of Congress Cataloging-in-Publication Data

Green, Carl R.
The mystery of fortune-telling / Carl R. Green and William R. Sanford ; illustrated by Gerald Kelley.
p. cm. — (Investigating the unknown)
Rev. ed. of: Fortune telling.
Summary: "Examines fortune-telling, including a brief history of it, the different methods, famous fortune-tellers, and a scientific look at predicting the future"—Provided by publisher.
Includes bibliographical references (p.) and index.
ISBN 978-0-7660-3819-6
1. Fortune-telling.—Juvenile literature. I. Sanford, William R. (William Reynolds), 1927– II. Kelley, Gerald. III. Green, Carl R. Fortune telling. IV. Title.
BF1861.G74 2012
133.3—dc22 2010031033

Paperback ISBN 978-1-59845-304-1

052011 Leo Paper Group, Heshan City, Guangdong, China

Printed in China

10 9 8 7 6 5 4 3 2 1

To Our Readers: We have done our best to make sure all Internet addresses in this book were active and appropriate when we went to press. However, the author and the publisher have no control over and assume no liability for the material available on those Internet sites or on other Web sites they may link to. Any comments or suggestions can be sent by e-mail to comments@enslow.com or to the address on the back cover.

Illustration Credits: Corel Corporation, p. 20; Everett Collection, pp. 16, 41; Keystone / Eyedea / Everett Collection, p. 15; © Photos.com, pp. 19, 30 (left), 40 (top); Shutterstock.com, pp. 1, 4, 6, 21, 25, 26, 30 (right), 31, 35; U.S. Army, p. 42.

Original Illustrations: © 2010 Gerald Kelley, www.geraldkelley.com, pp. 9, 12, 27, 38, 40 (bottom).

Cover Illustration: Shutterstock.com (Fortune-teller staring into a crystal ball).

Contents

Authors' Note

Thanks to science, many of nature's great mysteries have been solved. Do you want to know about earthquakes or earthworms? There's an expert somewhere who can answer most of your questions. But wouldn't this be a boring world if we knew all there is to know? Perhaps that's why people want to believe that the mind does possess mysterious powers.

In this series, you'll learn about these mysteries of the unknown:

- ✦ *The Mystery of Fortune-Telling*
- ✦ *Astonishing Mind Powers*
- ✦ *The Mysterious Secrets of Dreams*
- ✦ *Amazing Out-of-Body Experiences*
- ✦ *Discovering Past Lives*
- ✦ *Sensing the Unknown*

Do such mysteries truly exist? Some people say yes, others say no. Once you've studied both sides of the debate, you can decide for yourself. Along the way, keep one important thought in mind. In this field, it is often hard to separate the real from the fake. It pays to be skeptical when setting out to explore the mysteries of the unknown.

Gazing Into a Murky Future

What does the future hold? The question is as old as the human race. In early days, people asked priests and shamans. Religions honored prophets who brought God's word. The quest for answers has gone on and on.

Over the centuries, psychics found "foolproof" methods for predicting the future. Palm readers found fate in the palm of one's hand. Fortune-tellers gazed deep into crystal balls. Teenagers and grandparents alike looked for clues in tarot cards. Old methods grew and new ones appeared.

Astrology emerged as the queen of fortune-telling. Millions shared the belief that the movements of the heavenly bodies ruled their lives. Trust in the stars did not stop with the common people. The rich and powerful went to astrologers, too. Adolf Hitler, the German dictator during World War II, was one of them. His interest began long before his rise to power.

In 1923, psychic Elsbeth Ebertin was asked to cast Hitler's horoscope. Starting with Hitler's birthday, April 20, 1889, she made her forecast: "A man of action . . . can expose himself to personal danger by . . . uncautious action," she wrote. "He is destined to play a 'Führer-role' in future battles." A few months later, Hitler touched off a short-lived revolt by hoodlums who belonged to his Nazi Party. The police picked him up and sent him to jail.[1]

Useful Definitions

A full list of fortune-telling systems would fill dozens of pages. Here are some of the most common:

astrology—The belief that the movements of the heavenly bodies influence our lives. Astrologers chart these influences by mapping the positions of the sun, moon, and planets at given times.

I Ching—A Chinese system of foretelling the future. The I Ching's predictions are based on patterns chosen by tossing coins or sticks.

numerology—The belief that everything in the universe can be expressed by numbers. Numerologists claim that your character and future are determined by your name and birth numbers.

palmistry—The belief that both character and future can be read "in the palm of your hand." Palmists study the shape of the hand as well as the mounts and lines of the palm.

scrying—A fortune-telling method in which fortune-tellers gaze into a shiny surface until a "vision" appears deep within. These visions, they say, allow them to make predictions and solve problems.

tarot—A deck of seventy-eight cards much favored by fortune-tellers. Tarot readers claim that the fall of the cards reveals answers about the future.

Ebertin's seemingly pinpoint forecast helped turn Hitler into a fan. In 1939, a Swiss newspaper wrote: "It is not by accident that [the Führer's] coups are all made in the month of March. Before striking, he chooses the most favorable time indicated by the stars." At crucial times during the war, British leaders asked their own astrologers to cast Hitler's horoscope. Careful study of these horoscopes gave army planners useful clues about the timing of German attacks.[2]

During the Korean War, a Texan named Betty M. feared for her soldier husband. On an impulse, she went to see a psychic. Madame Lil said she would answer three questions for five dollars. Betty asked only one. "Will Dave come home safely from the war?"

Betty M. went to see Madame Lil to ask if her soldier husband would return from the war. The fortune-teller assured Betty that Dave would come home safely. Did Madame Lil see the answer in her crystal ball or was she a fake?

The fortune-teller stared into her crystal ball. After a long pause, she said, "He will fight often and kill many foes. But he will come home safely when the war is done."

Betty left the trailer feeling that all would be well. The five dollars was well spent, she thought. Then a letter came from the Far East. Dave wrote that he would soon be shipped home. He would not be sent into combat after all. Betty began to wonder if the fortune-teller had been a fake.

Her sister, Patsy, laughed. "If Madame Lil can foretell the future, why is she living in a trailer? Why doesn't she use her crystal ball to make a killing at the racetrack?"[3]

Are all fortune-tellers fakes and frauds? Clearly, many are. Even so, people still pay good money to have their fortunes told. They seem to think that fortune-tellers have powers the skeptics cannot explain.

A Brief History of Fortune-Telling

Jenny pushed her cherry pits into a pile. "Now, I'll find out who I'll marry," she told her brothers. "Rich man, poor man, beggar man, thief," she sang as she counted the pits. Now there were only five left. "Doctor, lawyer, Indian chief. Tinker—and tailor! The cherry pits say I'm going to marry a tailor," she laughed.[1]

Does counting cherry pits sound a little silly? Maybe yes, maybe no. People have always studied chance events in hopes of catching a glimpse of the future. They have plucked flower petals, studied tea leaves, and thrown dice. Often they put their faith in priests and seers.

Six thousand years ago in what is now Iraq, Chaldean priests looked for omens in nature. Perhaps they saw flocks of birds flying in circles at sunset. Could this mean the gods were planning to send a plague? Egypt's priests went to sleep hoping to catch dreams sent by the gods. The Bible tells of the pharaoh who dreamed of seven lean cattle that ate seven fat ones. That dream stumped even the wisest of his priests. Only a Hebrew named Joseph could make sense of the dream. It was a warning from God, Joseph said. Seven good years would be followed by seven years of famine.[2]

In ancient Greece, kings and peasants alike flocked to the oracle of Delphi. All gave gifts to the gods and prayed for answers to their questions. Inside the temple, a priestess chewed bay leaves and breathed a strong vapor. As she fell into a trance, her hair stood on end. She began to babble. A priest stood by to interpret her garbled words for the waiting people.[3]

In ancient Greece, many people visited the oracle of Delphi, hoping that their questions and prayers would be answered.

A seer warned Julius Caesar, "Beware the Ides [15th] of March." The Roman ruler listened, shrugged, and went to the Forum on that fatal day. As he climbed the steps, a group of plotters stabbed him to death. In fact, Caesar went to his doom doubly warned. His wife had dreamed of his death the night before. She, too, urged him not to go to the Forum.

Fortune-tellers appear in all times and places. Two thousand years ago in northern Europe, Druid priests locked thieves in wicker cages. The priests then burned their unfortunate victims on huge bonfires. Why were they so cruel? The Druids thought that the gods spoke to them in the screams of the prisoners.

Half a world away and centuries later, Aztec astrologers helped bring down their own culture. The cause lay in their belief that the god Quetzalcoatl would return in what they called a "One Reed" year. In 1519, a One Reed year in the Aztec calendar, Hernán Cortés landed in Mexico. Was the Spaniard, with his light skin and red beard, a man or a god? The Aztecs could not be sure, so they treated him like a god. Using his advantage to the fullest, Cortés and his small army of Spanish soldiers and Indian allies conquered the mighty Aztec empire.[4]

Beginning in the 1700s, stores sold books of forecasts known as almanacs. U.S. farmers were surprised one year when the Old Farmer's Almanac predicted a summer snowfall. In truth, the forecast was the result of a printer's error. That fact was ignored when snow did fall in northern New York State that summer.

Today, fortune-tellers still command notice. Perhaps the best known was Jeane Dixon. When Jeane was a child, a fortune-teller gave her a crystal ball. The lines in your hand tell me you will become a great seer, the fortune-teller told her. Soon, people were coming to the girl to ask for advice about the future.

In the fall of 1963, Jeane told friends that someone would shoot President John F. Kennedy. On November 19, she "saw" Kennedy dying from a head wound. Three days later, she said at breakfast, "This is the day—this is the day. It has to happen." She said the killer's name had

Aztec astrologers made predictions that helped destroy their own culture. In the same year that Hernán Cortés arrived, the Aztecs saw a fiery comet flash across the sky. To the people of Mexico, this was a bad omen. This illustration shows the Emperor Montezuma watching the fateful comet light up the sky above his palace.

Should I? Or Should I Not?

Need an answer, but can't afford a fortune-teller? Why not do it yourself? First, state your question so it can be answered with a yes or no. Don't ask, "Which CD should I buy?" Make it, "Should I buy Puppy Love's new CD?" Then try one of these techniques:

- ✦ Cut ten 5-by-5-inch slips of paper. Write "yes" on five and "no" on five. Fold the papers, put them in a box, and shake the box. Close your eyes, repeat your question, and draw one of the papers. The word you see written there is your answer.
- ✦ Do you have a pond or lake nearby? Repeat your question as you throw a rock into the water. Next, count the ripples that spread out from the splash. An even number means yes. An odd number means no.
- ✦ Divide an 8-inch circle into four equal parts. Write "yes" in parts one and three, "no" in parts two and four. Now tie a small weight to a string. Holding the string with both hands, center the weight over the circle. Concentrate on your question. As you do so, the weight will start to swing in circles. Be patient. Soon it will settle into a side-to-side arc. The words it crosses will tell you what you want to know.

Can you trust any of these answers? Skeptics say you might as well flip a coin.

Fortune-teller Jeane Dixon accurately predicted the assassination of President John F. Kennedy. Here, Kennedy (back left in the car) enjoys the cheers of a Dallas crowd moments before he was shot and killed.

six letters, starting with an O and an S. A few hours later, on November 22, 1963, Lee Harvey Oswald shot the president.[5] Jeane's predictions appeared in many U.S. newspapers until her death on January 25, 1997.

Are there forces in nature that can explain a fortune-teller's success? Most scientists say no. They dismiss all fortune-tellers as fakes. Does the public care? Check the Internet. You will find page after page of listings and advertisements for "psychic advisers," "spiritual consultants," and the like. Clearly, there must be a demand for their services.

CHAPTER THREE

Searching the Skies for Answers

Perry M. was worried. This was the biggest soccer game of the year. As goalie for the Sharks, he knew the team was counting on him. Was he up to the challenge?

As Perry read the comics that morning, he noticed a box called *Daily Horoscope*. That was it! Maybe the stars would tell him what kind of game he would play. Perry found his birth sign, Aries. Then he read:

> *Aries (March 21–April 19):* Take a bold step into the future. Focus on knowledge that you can take risks—there is a safety net. A Libra will help you reach your goals.

Perry felt a surge of hope. He could afford to take risks today. The stars said he would triumph! The fact that Coach Kane was a Libra was the topper. "This game is in the bag," he told his mom.

As a matter of fact, the Sharks did win the league title that day. Perry did his part with three big saves in overtime. Later, Coach Kane scolded him for taking too many big risks. Perry just smiled. "I had a safety net," he said.[1]

Was Perry's big game "written in the stars"? Or was his confidence based on pure chance? People have relied on astrology ever since the first sky charts were drawn, thousands of years ago.

Astrologers study the movements of the sun, moon, planets, and stars. The position of these bodies at the time of your birth, they say, determines your fate. To believe in this theory, however, requires an act of faith. No hard proof exists to support these claims.

All early peoples thought Earth was fixed in place at the center of the universe. In the ancient Middle East, priests mapped the apparent movements of the planets and the brightest stars. Along with the sun and moon, the planets and stars became objects of worship. The priests believed their paths across the sky showed links with the past, present, and future.

In Babylon, the number system was based on twelve, not ten. Remnants of that old system can still be seen on our rulers and clocks. Easy-to-spot groups of stars (the constellations) marked the hours in the night sky. Each took a 120-minute hour to rise above the horizon. As a result, the early astrologers divided the sky into twelve parts. Each was named for the constellation that dominated it. Their charts also showed that the sun cuts a yearly path across these twelve parts.

In time, the data helped create a science called astronomy. Earth was found to be a planet that follows its own orbit around the sun. When early astronomers announced that the sun's path only changed as Earth's orbit shifted, astrologers ignored them. Today's astrologers still depend on charts that are five thousand years out of date.

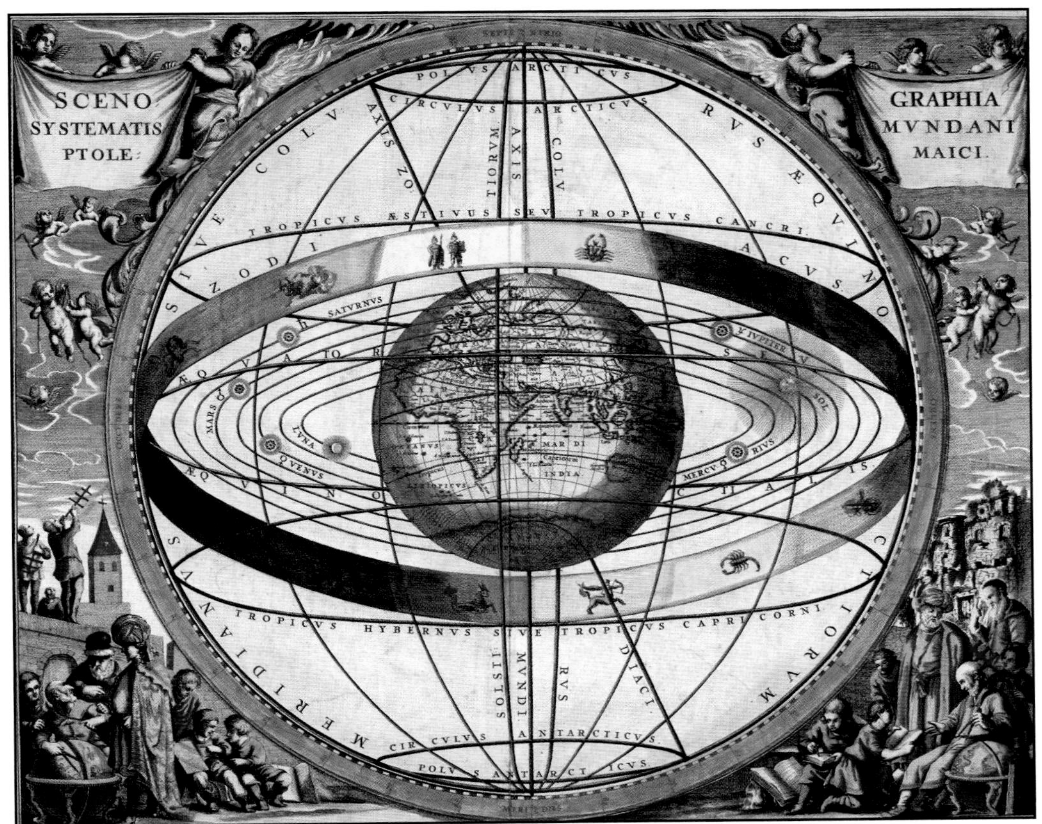

In ancient times, astronomers and astrologers believed that the universe revolved around the Earth. This seventeenth-century map shows the planets and stars revolving around what the map maker imagined was an Earth that dwarfed the other heavenly bodies.

The Greeks made their own changes to the old charts. They called the path formed by the sun's passage the zodiac. The constellations became the signs of the zodiac. In Babylon, the morning star had been known as Ishtar. The Greeks renamed it Aphrodite. Later, the Romans renamed it Venus. By then, each zodiac sign had been assigned its own set of behavioral traits. Were you born under the sign of Taurus (April 20–May 19)? Taureans are thought to be stubborn and generous. Well-organized Capricorns (December 22–January 20) are said to make good leaders.[3]

A Royal Horoscope

Charles, Prince of Wales, was born on November 14, 1948, under the sign of Scorpio. What kind of person is the man who may one day become king of England? Astrologers think they know the answer to that question.

Scorpios, they say, want to do something useful with their lives. Charles fits that description. He was born to take on a heavy burden of public service. His horoscope also shows that he needs to take risks. How does a prince take risks? Charles straps on a helmet and plays polo.

Charles's sun sign tells astrologers that he enjoys wealth and power. At the same time, his "moon in Taurus" pulls him close to nature. Charles resolves that conflict by using his prestige to protect the environment. Scorpios are also said to be cool under fire. Those who know him say that Charles meets that standard. Nothing in his horoscope, however, clearly predicted his marriage problems, or the tragic death of his ex-wife, Princess Diana, one year after their divorce.[2]

What if Charles had been born a few weeks later? Sagittarians (Nov. 22–Dec. 21) tend to be impulsive and full of energy. They are hard workers, anxious to get things done. Charles fits those traits, too. Skeptics remind us that each birth sign contains traits shared by many people. No horoscope, they insist, can predict the exact path a life will take.

Prince Charles playing polo.

Birth Sign	Dates	Character Traits
Aries	March 21–April 19	creative, quick-tempered, loyal
Taurus	April 20–May 19	stubborn, determined, generous
Gemini	May 20–June 20	adaptable, loving, confident
Cancer	June 21–July 22	sensitive, moody, loyal
Leo	July 23–Aug. 21	brave, suspicious, loves attention
Virgo	Aug. 22–Sept. 22	creative, versatile, good at details
Libra	Sept. 23–Oct. 22	understanding, imitative, original
Scorpio	Oct. 23–Nov. 21	strong-willed, blunt, fearless
Sagittarius	Nov. 22–Dec. 21	cheerful, energetic, impatient
Capricorn	Dec. 22–Jan. 20	scholarly, calm, well-organized
Aquarius	Jan. 21–Feb. 19	friendly, dignified, giving
Pisces	Feb. 20–March 20	modest, generous, cautious

What's your sign? Astrologers believe that your birth date helps determine your character traits and your destiny. Check out this chart to see if the character traits match up to the "real" you.

Astrologers admit that the forecasts found in newspapers are mostly for fun. If you want real insights, they say, pay a trained astrologer to cast your horoscope. Personal horoscopes take a number of factors into account. Exactly where on Earth were you born? What planet ruled the skies in the year of your birth? Someone born in 1980, for instance, is ruled by the moon. What planet controls the day of your birth? People born on Saturday are Saturn's children. Were you born "on the cusp"—in the first or last week of a sign? If so, you fall under the influence of the nearby sign, too.

Astrology tells us that people born on the same day share the same traits. Beatle John Lennon, born a Libra on October 9, won fame as a rock star. Why is it, then, that many Librans cannot carry a tune? True believers are not upset by such questions. They say that all Librans are born with a similar bundle of traits. As they grow, these traits are shaped by their specific life forces. We are all free to make as much of our lives as we will.

CHAPTER FOUR

Does the Future Lie in the Palm of Your Hand?

In ancient Greece, Hippocrates, the father of medicine, ordered his students to study palmistry. Modern doctors also find it useful to study their patients' hands. Research has found that liver disease, for example, shows up in the lines of the palm.

If your hands provide a blueprint of your health, can they also foretell your future? Once again, scientists say no. Palmists, however, say yes. Your hands, they claim, reveal both character and destiny.

Ancient cave paintings often show handprints next to drawings of deer and horses. Perhaps the cave dwellers thought the prints brought success in the hunt. The art of palmistry itself might have begun in India as far back as 3000 B.C. From there, it spread westward to Egypt and beyond. The Romani, or "Gypsies" as they are often called, a wandering people from India, brought the art to the West. Many palm readers wear gypsy dress, even though they are not true Gypsies.

If you go to a palmist (let's call her Madame Rose) for a reading, you may be in for a few surprises. First, Rose will look at much more than the lines in your palm. She will base her reading on four factors:

- ✦ The shape, color, and texture of your hand (fingers, nails, and palm)
- ✦ Fingerprints and skin patterns
- ✦ The way you hold your hands and fingers
- ✦ The lines and mounts[1]

Are you right-handed or left-handed? Palmists read the hand you use most often. If you ask, they will name each finger, line, and mount. The first finger, for instance, is named for Jupiter. The fold between fingers and thumb is called the Valley of the Sun. The fleshy pads on the palm have names like Mount of Apollo. The area at the base of the thumb is called the Mount of Venus. The hollow center of the palm is known as the Plain of Mars. The tips of the fingers are named for Pluto.

Do you have a well-shaped Jupiter finger? Palmists say you are cut out to be a leader. What if your Jupiter finger is crooked? That means someone or something is holding you back. The Plain of Mars, named for the Roman god of war, provides clues about a person's courage. The little (Mercury) finger relates to science and speech arts. Do you have a long, lean little finger? That means you are likely to be a witty speaker. People with short Mercury fingers are said to be shy and bashful.[2]

Madame Rose turns next to the lines on your palm. You can see that some of the lines stand out from the others. The strongest lines are the Life Line, the Head Line, the Heart Line, and the Line of Fate.

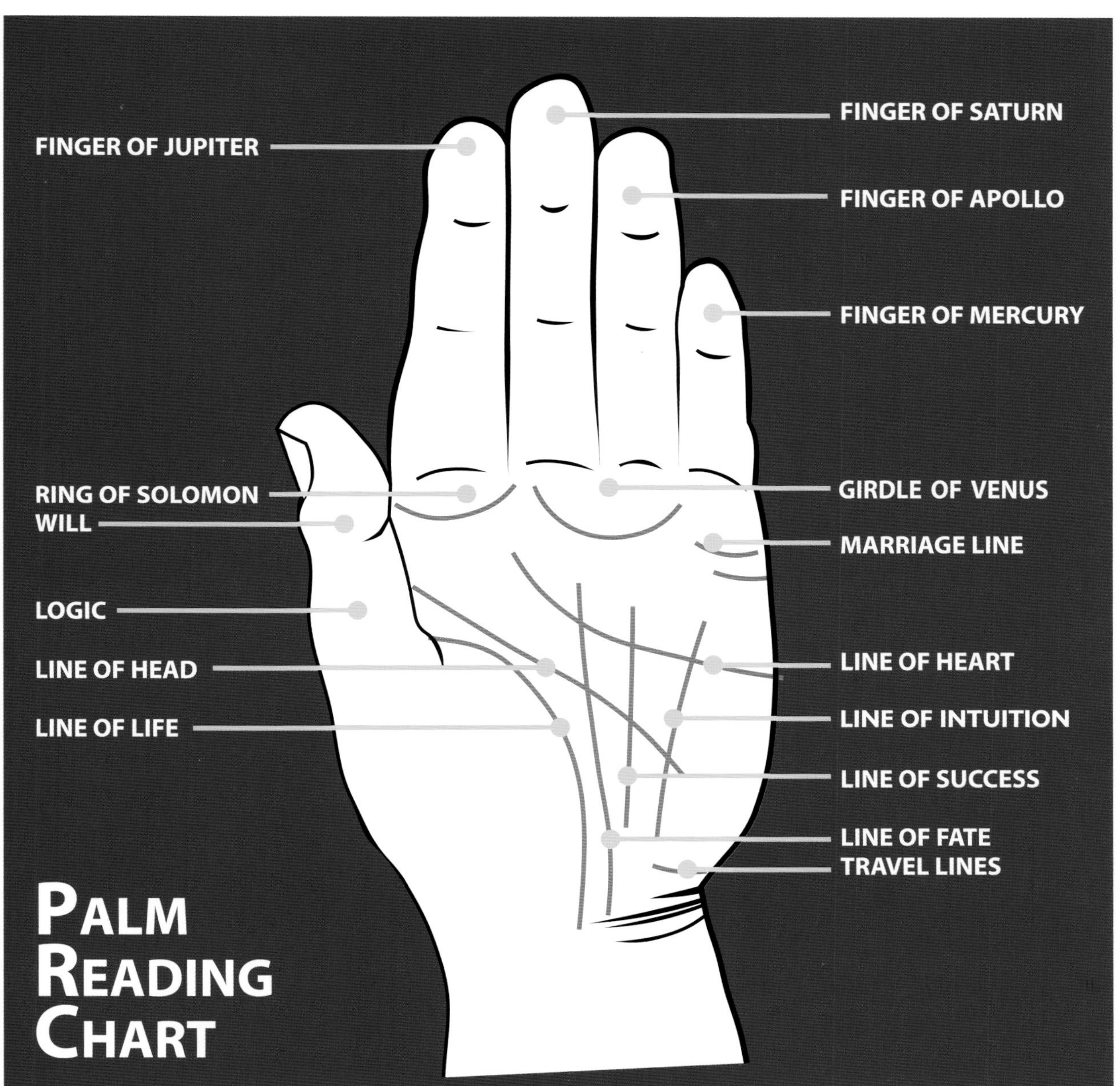

Palmists look at all parts of the hand when doing a reading. Each line and mount has a different meaning. Do you have a strong Heart Line? If so, a palmist would tell you that you can look forward to a happy love life.

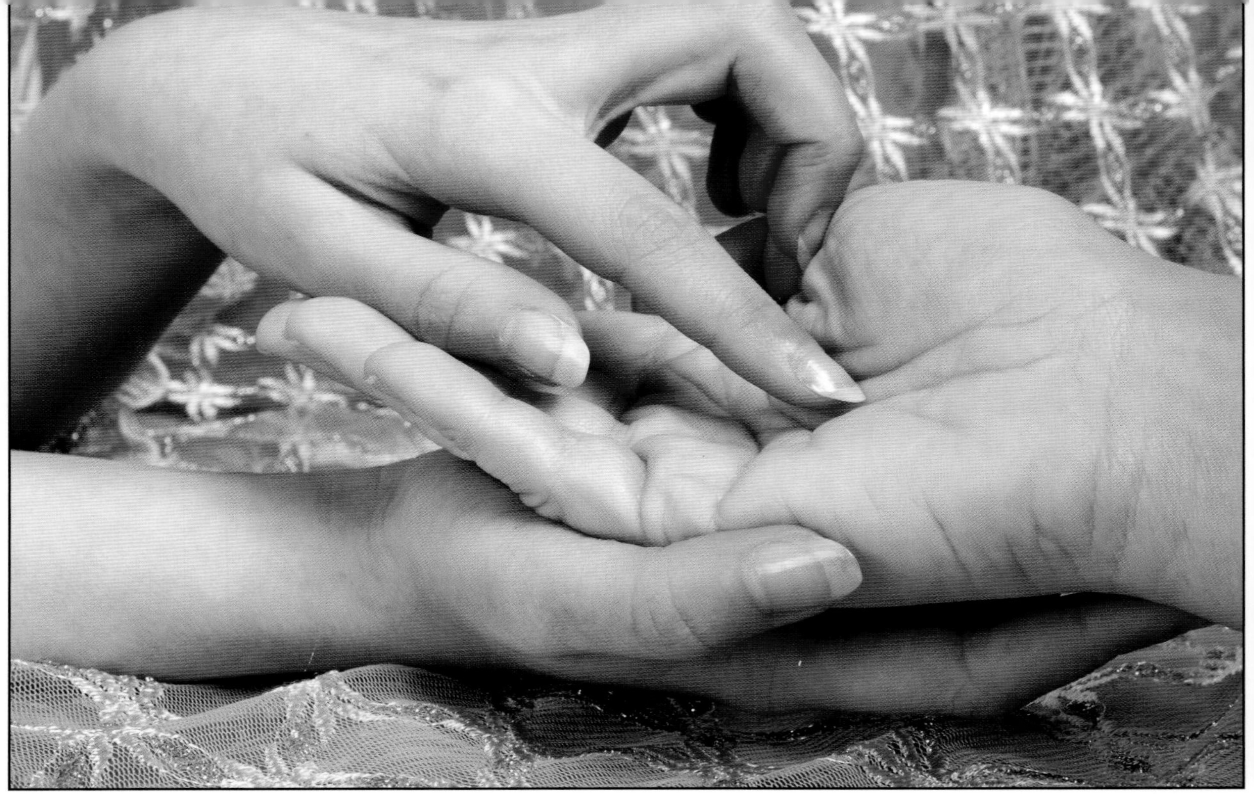

Palmists carefully trace the lines and mounts of your palm when they do a reading. Can you believe all the things a palmist tells you? That's up to you.

Your Life Line traces an arc from your wrist to just above the thumb. A long, solid line means a long and healthy life. A break in the line predicts a major illness. Does the Life Line form a chain? That suggests a nervous person. Is it deep and red? That's someone who tends to scorch the ears of others with angry outbursts.[3]

The Head Line cuts across the center of the palm to meet the Life Line. A clear, bold line stamps the person as a clear thinker. An upward curve suggests a talent for math and science. A downward curve leads one toward the arts. The Heart Line can be found just above the Head Line. A strong, clean line suggests a loving nature. Each break in the line

Your Body Has a Message for You?

The fortune-teller sees the future in the palm of your hand. Psychologist William Sheldon gave that belief a new spin. He taught that your whole body shapes your destiny.

All of us fit into one of three body types, Sheldon found. The endomorph, he said, has a soft, round body. The mesomorph lives inside a strong, athletic body. The ectomorph is tall, thin, and fragile. Although no one is a pure type, most people clearly fit into one of these three body types.

Sheldon matched behavior with each body type. Endomorphs, he said, enjoy parties, comfort, and good food. They are often slow to react and slow to anger. Mesomorphs love sports and games. They tend to be take-charge types. Ectomorphs are often shy and bookish. They would rather play chess than baseball.[4]

Scientists agree that Sheldon was at least half right. If the culture expects soft, pudgy people to be jolly, they learn to act the part. Parents who push a frail, thin child to star in sports may do more harm than good. But Sheldon was half wrong, too. Some ectomorphs excel on the basketball court. Gifted with height, they work to develop weight and strength. Whatever your body type, remember this: you are free to be the best you can be.

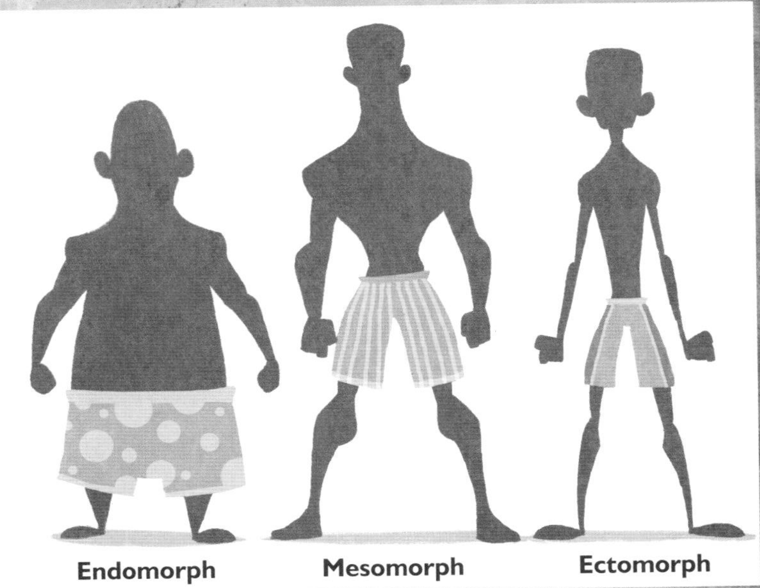

stands for an unhappy love affair. Do you have a star near your Heart Line? If so, you are destined to be lucky in love.[5]

Now Madame Rose studies your Line of Fate. This line runs upward from your wrist toward your middle (Saturn) finger. Breaks in this line stand for the normal ups and downs of life. Does your Line of Fate reach the Mount of Jupiter beneath the first finger? What luck! You will have success in all you do.[6]

Should you trust the palmist? It feels good when she says, "Great rewards await in your chosen field." But you know in your heart that success takes more than a strong Life Line. It requires hard work and talent, too.

CHAPTER FIVE

Three More Windows to the Future

How many methods of fortune-telling exist in today's world? The number must run into the hundreds. In this chapter, we will look at three of the most popular. They are the tarot, tea-leaf reading, and crystal-ball reading.

The Tarot

One of the most common fortune-telling methods is the tarot. No one knows where or when this colorful deck of 78 cards was first created. We do know that the tarot deck divides into three parts. The best known are the 22 picture cards called the Major Arcana. The 16 Court Cards and 40 Minor Arcana look much like a modern deck of cards.

Simple tarot readings rely on the Major Arcana. The reader begins by arranging the cards in a special pattern. Each card carries a message, but its meaning can be modified by nearby cards. As the pattern builds, your future comes into focus. Legend says that Napoleon, emperor of France, believed in the tarot. On the eve of the Battle of Waterloo, he

Legend tells us that Napoleon (left), emperor of France, believed in the tarot cards. The night before the Battle of Waterloo, during a tarot card reading, the ill-omened Tower turned up next to the Emperor. As the tarot predicted, Napoleon's army suffered a crushing defeat the following day.

saw the Tower turn up next to the Emperor. That was a bad omen. Napoleon knew that the Tower signals a coming defeat. Whether the story is true or not, he went on to lose the battle and his crown.[1]

Do you have a good memory and a feeling for people? If so, you can learn to read the tarot. Decks come with instructions that describe the layouts and the meanings of each card. Learning those meanings is only a start. A good reader studies each sitter and tailors the message to fit.

(Note: Custom says that it is bad luck to buy your own tarot deck. Ask a friend to buy it for you.)

Tea-Leaf Reading

Telling fortunes with tea leaves began in China. For many years, this form of fortune-telling was hugely popular in the United States. Zee James, wife of the famous outlaw Jesse James, was a skilled reader. Perhaps Zee forgot to read her tea leaves on April 3, 1882. That was the day that Bob Ford shot Jesse in the back of the head.[2]

The reader starts by making tea in a bell-shaped, smooth-sided white teacup. This is one time when tea bags will not do! If you are the sitter, think about a wish or a question while you drink the tea. When only a spoonful remains, swirl the cup three times to the left. Pour out the last drops, leaving the tea leaves behind. Now it is the reader's turn. The first "picture" formed by the tea leaves is the answer to your wish or question.

Can tea leaves truly predict the future? This woman reads her tea leaves in a traditional teahouse.

A Quick Tour of Offbeat Fortune-Telling Methods

Fortune-tellers never seem to run out of ideas. Here are some offbeat techniques:

Aeromancy is the study of strange happenings in the sky. Where the astronomer sees a comet, the fortune-teller sees an omen of disaster. An eclipse might be read as a sign of floods or earthquakes to come.

Bibliomancy requires only a book and an open mind. Pick any book that has meaning for you (many people use the Bible). Close your eyes and think about your question. As you do so, open the book at random. Point to a spot on the page and open your eyes. The words you read will provide your answer.

Hydromancy makes use of a pool of water (a puddle will do). Throw three pebbles into the water and study the pattern they make. You may find the answer to your question there.

Oomancy uses raw eggs to tell fortunes. The questioner lets three or four drops of egg white fall into a jar of water. When wispy shapes appear, the reader tries to make sense of them. As with tea leaves, a ring means marriage. A ship predicts a journey.

As the reader turns the cup, further shapes become clear. These predict the future.

What do you see in the cup? A ring speaks of a marriage. Anchors and airplanes predict a journey. Swords and crosses tell of trouble to come. Triangles and stars mean good luck is on the way. Will your wish come true? Look for three dots in a row.[3]

Some people start each day by reading their own tea leaves. Check your library for books that teach this fortune-telling art.

Crystal-Ball Reading

Long before glass was invented, priests tried to glimpse the future in pools of water. If they stared long enough, pictures that foretold coming events seemed to appear. This fortune-telling method is called scrying. In time, crystal balls replaced the pools of water.

Crystal-ball readers claim a high ranking among fortune-tellers. It is said that only clairvoyants can find answers in a crystal ball. Clairvoyants "see at a distance" without using the normal senses. The crystal ball itself is not magic. Its job is to focus the clairvoyant's powers.[4]

You do not need a crystal ball to test your own powers. Use a mirror, a bowl of water, or a shiny piece of metal. Go into a quiet room and pull the shades. Try to empty your mind of all thought as you stare into the shiny surface. Do you see something in the depths? What does it tell you? If nothing happens, try again a few days later. If you have the gift, the visions will come.

CHAPTER SIX

Hexagrams and Name Numbers

Two popular fortune-telling methods come down to us from ancient times. The Chinese developed a complex system called the I Ching. A system known as numerology began in ancient Greece.

The I Ching

The modern I Ching is based on sixty-four figures of six lines each. Each hexagram carries meanings that date back to the twelfth century B.C. Later, the great teacher Confucius added his own comments. Like the tarot, the I Ching does not give yes-and-no answers. Each of us must find our own meanings when reading the hexagrams.

To foretell the future, toss three coins six times. Some people use pennies. Others insist on Chinese coins. The fall of heads and tails yields six lines, either solid or broken. The hexagram created in this way must be studied for its relation to the seeker's question.

Teri K.'s coin tosses yielded the hexagram Kuai, or breakthrough. Since Teri was asking for advice about a possible love affair, Kuai was

The I Ching's 12 Most Important Hexagrams

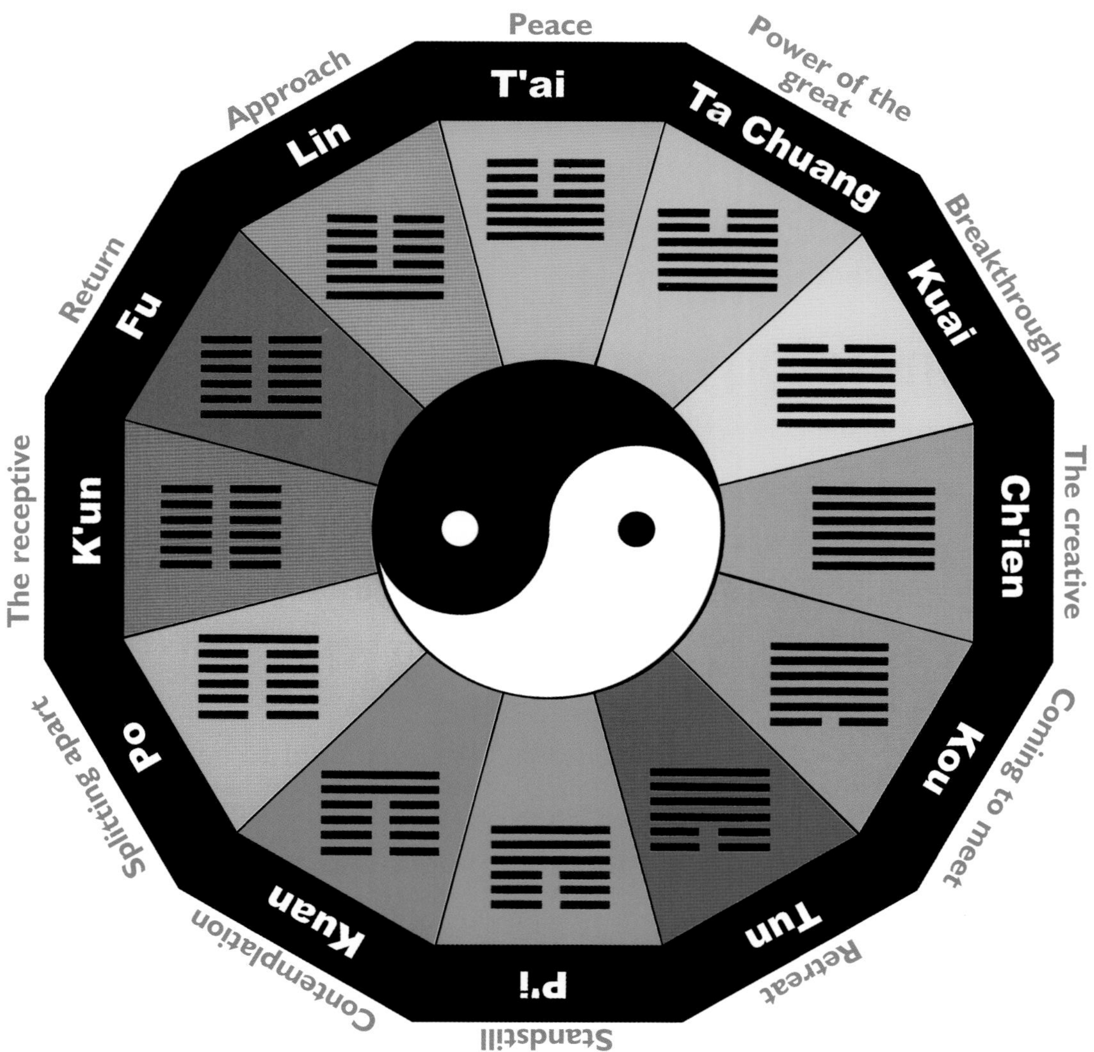

If you want to experiment with I Ching, toss three coins six times. The first toss creates the top line, and so on. If all three coins turn up heads (or tails), draw a solid line. A mixed toss gives you a broken line. After you finish the tosses, look at this chart to see what your hexagram means.

a good sign. The text of the I Ching told her, "A breakthrough in your relationship is coming." If Teri had drawn the Tun, she would not have been so pleased. Tun stands for retreat.[1]

Scientist Lyall Watson was a fan of the I Ching. Watson guessed that the fall of the coins is influenced by the unconscious mind. "There is nothing in the fall of the coins or in the text of the book that is not already in you," he wrote. The I Ching, he concluded, taps self-knowledge that already exists.[2]

Numerology

Numerologists claim that their system of fortune-telling makes the most sense of all. The universe, they explain, is built on mathematical principles. From atoms to zebras, all things can be expressed by numbers. The trick lies in reducing names, birth dates, and other data to simple numbers. When you do so, the theory says, a person's character and destiny stand revealed.

The Greek mathematician Pythagoras is thought to be the founder of numerology. It was Pythagoras who focused on the numbers one to nine. He reduced larger numbers to a single digit by adding each digit to the next. Thus, 456 has no special meaning. But 4 + 5 + 6 = 15, and 1 + 5 = 6. A six, the numerology charts say, suggests luck, balance, and harmony.

Want to give the system a test? The first step is to reduce your name to a number. It is best to work with the name that gives the best sense of who you are. Some people choose the full name they sign on checks and contracts. Others use their nicknames. Here's a table that will help you convert your name to a number.[3]

1	2	3	4	5	6	7	8	9
A	B	C	D	E	F	G	H	I
J	K	L	M	N	O	P	Q	R
S	T	U	V	W	X	Y	Z	

When Ann Marie Smith used this table, she found she was a nine. Her first name, for example, became A=1, N=5, and N=5. Her math looked like this when she changed each letter to a number:

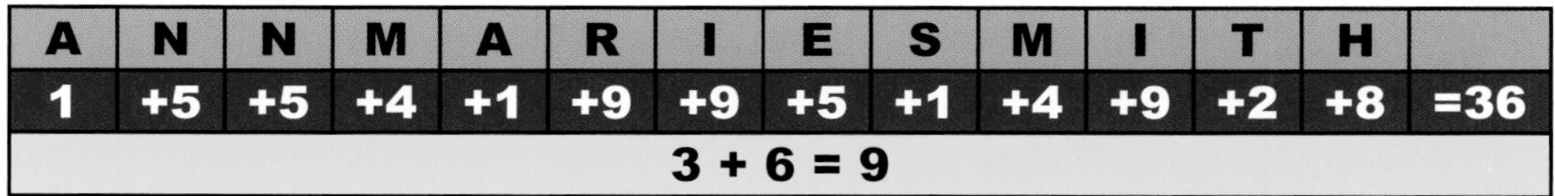

A	N	N	M	A	R	I	E	S	M	I	T	H	
1	+5	+5	+4	+1	+9	+9	+5	+1	+4	+9	+2	+8	=36
3 + 6 = 9													

Now, convert your own name to its base number. What does it say about you? Here's a simple chart to get you started.

1 = expressive, creative
2 = friendly, brave, active
3 = ambitious, fair, reliable
4 = outspoken, kind, independent
5 = energetic, adventuresome
6 = lucky in money and love
7 = sensitive, sharing, nature-lover
8 = kind, lovable, level-headed
9 = strong, proud, forceful[4]

The "master numbers" 11, 22, and 33 are never reduced to single digits. People with these name numbers are said to be highly advanced in the spirit realm. Numerologists add that changing your name also changes your traits. Just do not expect the change to take place overnight. It may help to compare your number with those of your friends. An outspoken 4 and a forceful 9, the chart warns, can expect to clash.

Numerologists believe that all things can be expressed in numbers, even your name. They believe the letters of your name can be converted to a base number and that this number reveals your character traits. Imagine going to a party where everyone wore a number instead of a name tag! Would you expect Guest 3 and Guest 8 to get along well together?

CHAPTER SEVEN

Science Tackles the Fortune-Teller

The story made headlines in the 1980s. Nancy Reagan, wife of the president of the United States, had asked an astrologer for help. Did that mean that President Reagan took advice from fortune-tellers? The White House rushed to assure the public that the answer was no. Only Reagan's schedule, aides said, had been influenced by Nancy's astrologer.[1]

The news opened a widespread debate. As talk shows chewed at the issue, three sides emerged.

First, many people approved of Nancy's actions. In their minds, astrology is as real as the force of gravity. When pressed, they remind skeptics that the moon affects the life cycle of simple life-forms. A surge in sunspots can change rainfall patterns. Faith in astrology helps these people cope with their doubts and fears.

During the 1800s, phrenology supplied that same comfort. Phrenologists claimed that destiny lay in the shape of one's skull. Will your sister grow up to be a doctor or a lawyer? Measure the proper

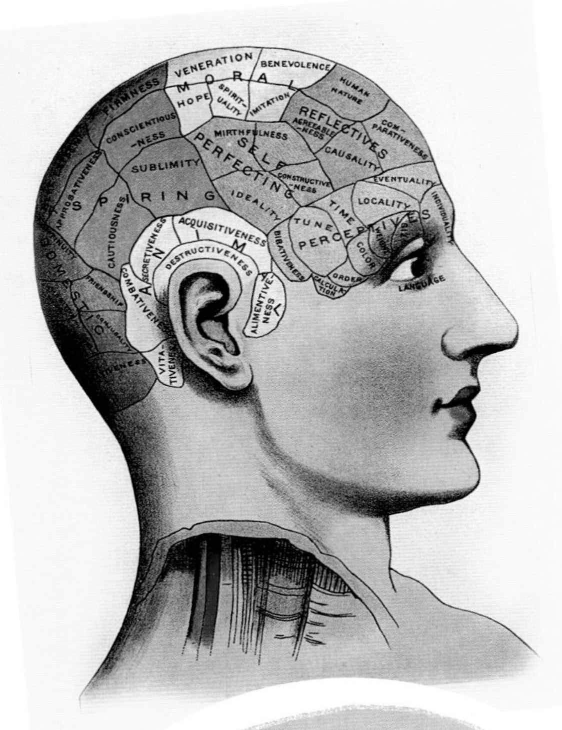

Phrenologists once believed that character and abilities are revealed in the shape of one's skull. Detailed "maps" guided their search for clues as to what a person was capable of achieving.

places on her skull and you will know. In time, phrenology was proven false. That did not change the minds of true believers. They claimed to see the truth of phrenology in their own lives.

Second, millions of people view fortune-telling as a pleasant pastime. Think of it, they say, as a sort of mental bubble gum. It does not nourish, but neither does it do harm. Why not start the day by glancing at your horoscope? Once in a while, those vague forecasts come true! When they do, people feel both amused and comforted. When they fail, nothing is lost.

Mental health experts see very little harm in this habit.

Although phrenology has been proven false, true believers still exist. What do you think? Is it possible that your future can be read in the bumps on your head?

Can We Talk to Spirits?

Seven men and women sit around a table, holding hands. Rather than consult a palmist or a tarot reader, they have put their faith in a medium. They turn toward Madame Chan as she asks for silence. "I will now call on the spirits of the dead," she says. As she slips into a trance, ghostly raps echo through the room. The séance is under way.

A clock ticks off long, tense moments. Then the woman speaks again. "I am Thul," a deep voice says. "I am Madame Chan's spirit contact. Tell me what you want."

One by one, the people in the group ask their questions. Many want to know if their dead loved ones are happy. Others ask about the future. New spirits arrive to assure the questioners that all is well. "Keep your money in safe stocks and bonds," Thul tells one man. "Do not trust one who claims to be your friend."

Séances like this still go on, but belief in spirits has fallen. Too many mediums have been exposed as frauds. The magician Harry Houdini once offered hard cash to any medium he could not expose as a fake. No one ever collected, though many tried. Before his death, Houdini also promised to "come back" if he could. Efforts are still being made to reach him, but so far without success.

Magician Harry Houdini exposed many mediums as frauds. This poster from 1909 advertises a magic show in which Houdini proved that mediums do not converse with spirits of the dead.

Can psychics truly predict natural disasters? Sometimes they guess right, but most of their predictions misfire. Even if fortune-tellers had correctly foreseen the earthquake that reduced many of Haiti's buildings to rubble in January 2010, their warnings likely would have been ignored.

The world does seem to be speeding out of control at times. What can you do about famine in Africa or drive-by shootings in Houston? At times, it seems simpler to consult the tarot. The danger lies, the experts say, in letting fortune-tellers make your life-shaping decisions for you.

A third approach involves hard science. Let's put fortune-telling to the test, the scientist says. Here are the results of several studies:

- Researchers showed each subject a stack of horoscopes. An astrologer had prepared one of them based on data taken from that subject. The others were filled with statements that could apply to anyone. Pick the horoscope that "fits you exactly," the subjects were told. They tried—and guessed wrong far more often than they guessed right.

- ✦ Twenty-seven psychics predicted the date and place of 240 earthquakes. A control group made their own random guesses. At the end of the study, the researchers checked the results. In the contest between psychics and guessers, the guessers won.
- ✦ Researchers checked out 3,011 forecasts made by astrologers. Only 11 percent of the forecasts came true. Many of the "hits" were clearly based on guesswork. A typical forecast: "A disaster will hit the East Coast this spring."[2]

Fortune-tellers ignore such studies. No test is perfect, they say. We know, they add, that the signs are never wrong. It is human beings who fail to read them correctly. Fortune-telling survives because it is more art than science. As it has for thousands of years, it appeals to the heart, not the head.

Chapter Notes

Chapter 1. Gazing Into a Murky Future

1. Ellic Howe, *Astrology—A Recent History, Including the Untold Story of Its Role in World War II* (New York: Walker & Company, 1967), p. 92.

2. Ibid., pp. 209–210, 235.

3. Personal experience as reported by P. N. Partin, 1951, Longview, Texas.

Chapter 2. A Brief History of Fortune-Telling

1. Personal observation as reported by Ren Sanford, September 1992, Kamuela, Hawaii.

2. Holy Bible, Genesis 41 (AV).

3. Alvin Schwartz, *Telling Fortunes* (New York: J. B. Lippincott, 1987), pp. 72–73.

4. Justine Glass, *They Foresaw the Future: The Story of Fulfilled Prophecy* (New York: G. P. Putnam's Sons, 1969), pp. 84–87.

5. Ibid., pp. 223–225.

Chapter 3. Searching the Skies for Answers

1. Personal experience of one of the authors, November 1976, Rancho Palos Verdes, California.

2. Paul Wright, *Astronomy in Action* (Sebastopol, Calif.: CRCS Publications, 1989), pp. 56–57.

3. Richard Cavendish, ed., *Man, Myth & Magic, vol. 1* (New York: Marshall Cavendish Corp., 1970), pp. 149–150.

Chapter 4. Does the Future Lie in the Palm of Your Hand?

1. Lori Reid, *How to Read Hands* (Wellingborough, England: Aquarian Press, 1985), p. 14.

2. Ibid., pp. 63–69.

3. Jagat S. Bright, *The Dictionary of Palmistry* (New York: Bell Publishing, 1958), p. 71.

4. Carl R. Green and William R. Sanford, *Psychology: A Way to Grow* (New York: Amsco School Publications, 1983), pp. 152–153.

5. Alvin Schwartz, *Telling Fortunes* (New York: J. B. Lippincott, 1987), pp. 51–52.

6. Bright, p. 71.

Chapter 5. Three More Windows to the Future

1. Margaret Baldwin, *Fortune Telling* (New York: Julian Messner, 1984), p. 10.

2. Ibid., p. 86.

3. Alvin Schwartz, *Telling Fortunes* (New York: J. B. Lippincott, 1987), pp. 29–31.

4. Baldwin, pp. 61–62.

Chapter 6. Hexagrams and Name Numbers

1. Carl R. Green and William R. Sanford, *Psychology: A Way to Grow* (New York: Amsco School Publications, 1983), p. 438.

2. Lyall Watson, *Supernature: A Natural History of the Supernatural* (London: Coronet Books, 1973), p. 302.

3. Rosemary Ellen Guiley, *Harper's Encyclopedia of Mystical & Paranormal Experience* (New York: HarperCollins, 1991), pp. 409–410.

4. *Personality Profile* (New York: Scholastic Magazines, 1976), p. 2.

Chapter 7. Science Tackles the Fortune-Teller

1. *The Americana Annual*, 1989 (Danbury, Conn.: Grolier Enterprises, 1989), p. 553.

2. Carol Tavris, "Astrology Thrives on the Gullibility Gene," *Los Angeles Times* (January 24, 1986), Opinion Section, p. 6.

Glossary

astrology—The belief that the movements of the heavenly bodies influence our lives.

clairvoyant—Someone who claims the ability to perceive events that take place beyond the range of the normal senses.

Druids—Priests of early Britain and Ireland who claimed mastery of the art of foretelling the future.

fortune-teller—Someone who claims to be able to give advice about the past, present, and future.

horoscope—An astrological diagram of the positions of the sun, moon, and planets at the moment of a person's birth.

I Ching—A Chinese system of foretelling the future.

medium—Someone who claims to be able to contact the spirits of the dead.

numerology—The belief that everything in the universe can be expressed in numbers.

omen—An event that can be seen as predicting future events, good or bad.

oracle—In ancient times, a wise man or woman who claimed the ability to predict the future.

palmistry—The belief that a person's character and future can be read in the lines, mounts, and shape of the hand.

pharaoh—The all-powerful god-kings of ancient Egypt.

phrenology—The fortune-telling art that reveals a person's abilities and interests by "reading" the contours of his or her skull.

prophet—A wise man or woman through whom God (or the gods) reveals the future.

psychic—Someone who claims powers that cannot be explained by natural laws.

scrying—A fortune-telling method that uses a crystal ball or mirror to foretell the future.

séance—A meeting at which a medium tries to help people contact the spirits of the dead.

seer—Someone who has the gift of prophecy or clairvoyance.

shaman—A priest or medicine man who is thought to possess healing powers.

skeptic—Someone who questions widely accepted beliefs or theories.

tarot—A deck of seventy-eight cards much favored by fortune-tellers.

unconscious mind—The mind's secret storehouse of feelings, thoughts, and memories.

zodiac—The yearly "circle of life" taken by the sun as it moves across the twelve astrological signs.

Further Reading

Books

Austin, Joanne P. *ESP, Psychokinesis, and Psychics*. New York: Chelsea House Publishers, 2008.

Krohn, Katherine. *Fortune-Telling*. Detroit: KidHaven Press, 2007.

McCormick, Lisa Wade. *Psychic Powers*. Mankato, Minn.: Capstone Press, 2010.

Place, Robert M. *Astrology and Divination*. New York: Chelsea House Publishers, 2008.

Walker, Kathryn. *Mysterious Predictions*. New York: Crabtree Publishing Co., 2010.

Internet Addresses

Disney Family Fun: Predict the Future
<http://familyfun.go.com/playtime/predict-the-future-705237/>

National Aeronautics and Space Administration (NASA): What's Your Sign?
<http://spaceplace.nasa.gov/en/kids/st6starfinder/st6starfinder2.shtml>

Unexplained Mysteries: Paranormal Phenomena and the World's Greatest Unexplained Mysteries
<http://www.unexplained-mysteries.com/>

Index